I JUST WANT TO SHARE

Vivian Brazil
Brazil like the country not like the nut!

JAZZI CREATIONS PUBLISHING

I Just Want To Share

ISBN: 978-0-9965975-0-0
LCCN: 2015914065

Copyright ©2015 by Vivian Brazil

No part of this book may be reproduced or transmitted in any form or by any means electronic or mechanical, including photocopying, recording, or by any information storage and retrieval system, without permission in writing from the author, except for the use of brief quotations in a book review.

Printed in the United States of America

Published by:
Jazzi Creations Self-Publishing Service
P.O. Box 490520
Chicago, Illinois 60649
Website: www.jazzicreations.com

Senior Editor: J. D. Cooper
Copy Editor: Relana Johnson
Proofreader Khiry Vanallen

Table Of Contents

ACKNOWLEDGMENTS		i
INTRODUCTION		ii
CHAPTER 1	REVERSE MORTGAGE	9
CHAPTER 2	PREFERRED HOMEMAKER PROGRAM	19
CHAPTER 3	NETWORKING	23
CHAPTER 4	VOLUNTEERING	33
CHAPTER 5	ADVICE & SUGGESTIONS	39
CHAPTER 6	REFLECTIONS	45
CHAPTER 7	55 THINGS I'VE LEARNED	51
CHAPTER 8	LAUGHTER FOR THE SOUL	61
CHAPTER 9	LIFE PICK UPS FROM BRAZIL LIKE THE COUNTRY	77
CHAPTER 10	APPENDIX	101
	CONCLUSION	129

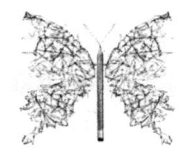

ACKNOWLEDGMENTS

First and foremost, I would like to thank God for my existence and for giving me the inspiration to write, ***I Just Want to Share.***

I would like to thank my mother, Ruth Webb, and my father Willie Webb (deceased) for being the channel through which I entered this world.

I want to thank my brother, Wilbert Webb (deceased), and sister, Sherice Webb for being in my life as my siblings.

I want to thank my daughter, Yvonne Lewis for being a marvelous daughter, and a great mother to my grandsons, Paul and Mario. I want to thank my son-in-law, Stan Lewis, for making my daughter happy.

Also, thanks to my nephews, Terrence Ball and Kenton Bowens for seeing about their auntie.

I would also like to thank my mentors, Cuttie Bacon III and G. Drew Williams for their guidance and knowledge with helping me to write this book.

Thanks to Carolann Jones for her input and Robert Pairs for the concept and design of my book cover and the initial editing of the manuscript.

Finally, thank you to all who have helped me with various ideas, suggestions, jokes and quotes.

Introduction

I am Vivian Brazil, that's BRAZIL like the COUNTRY, not like the NUT. I was born in Chicago, IL and raised on the south side in the Englewood area. I attended Bass and Beale grade schools and graduated from Parker High School. I worked for the United States Postal Service for thirty-five years in the capacity of Clerk, Postal Resource Worker, Classroom Instructor, and Lead Trainer.

I am the mother of one daughter, Yvonne Lewis, and grandmother to two grandsons, Paul and Mario. Currently, I am my ninety-four-year-old mother, Ruth's preferred homemaker. Also, I am Chairman of the Entertainment Committee for the South Suburban Postal Retirees, a member of the Saul Hall Mixed Bowling League, and Ace's Business Network A'fair (ABNA). I have faithfully attended the American Clergy Leadership Conference (ACLC) monthly prayer breakfast for over three years, and I am a member of Operation Push. I am also an Independent Distributor for Shaklee all natural vitamins, supplements, skin care system and environmentally safe (green) household, and laundry products.

I Just Want To Share is a compilation of my experiences, thoughts, suggestions, motivation, and inspiration. In this book, I am sharing information to clear up some of the myths that I have heard throughout my life.

In this book I shed light on the preferred homemaker, it is a little-known program to take some of the pressure off the senior by doing simple housekeeping, shopping, and personal care tasks.

As a Networker since 1994, I want to share a few short tips that I have learned. Hopefully, something I say will enlighten you.

An acquaintance of mine calls me the "virtual volunteer" which is why I wanted to touch briefly on this topic. When I worked for the postal service, I volunteered for numerous committees. I also volunteered at Clara's House (a shelter for homeless and battered women and children). Also, the International Stevenson Foundation, (assisting ex-offenders and those who were in recovery), where I eventually became the Director. I am adding some of the ideas and awards I received to spark some ideas within you.

As a mother and grandmother, I share wisdom, advice, suggestions, and a couple of my daughter's and grandson's accomplishments. Since laughter is good for the soul, I added some humor to lighten up your day.

Last but not least, I am the author of *31 Life Pickups From Brazil like the Country* ©2009. I expanded them to well over 100. My Life Pickups were inspired by the fact that I take notes everywhere I go, whether it be in church service, funerals, seminars, prayer breakfasts or TV. I am also an avid reader. When I hear or read something inspiring, I write it down. So sit back, relax and enjoy, **I Just Want To Share.**

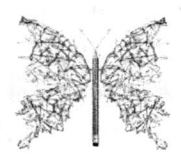

Chapter 1

REVERSE MORTGAGE

First of all, I am not saying that a reverse mortgage is for everyone. But for those who may be under financial stress, need major home repairs, or just some cash, this is a brief overview of one of your options.

A REVERSE MORTGAGE is a loan for senior homeowners that uses a part of the home's equity as collateral. The loan does not require repayment until the last surviving homeowner moves out of the property or dies. After that time, the estate has approximately six months to repay the loan or sell the home to pay off the balance.

The estate inherits the remaining equity. If the home sells for less than the balance, the property owner is not liable.

REVERSE MORTGAGE
vs
HOME EQUITY LOAN

Strict income requirements and credit scores determine the ability to get a home equity line of credit (HELOC) or a second mortgage. Homeowners must make monthly payments to repay the loans. With a reverse mortgage, there are no income or credit score requirements. The lender pays the homeowner instead of the owner making monthly payments to the lender.

The FHA (Federal Housing Authority) has a formula that takes into consideration, age, home appraisal value, and the current interest rate in determining the amount received. In essence, the more your home appraises for, the more you can get based on your age.

On traditional loans, homeowners are required to make monthly payments. Reverse mortgages have no monthly payments, but the homeowner handles maintenance, insurance, and real estate taxes.

ELIGIBILITY FOR A REVERSE MORTGAGE

The FHA requires that all homeowners are at least sixty-two (62) years of age to be eligible for a reverse mortgage. Ownership of the home is a requirement, and the home must not have any liens. If there are, the reverse mortgage can take care of them. Your mortgage balance may be paid off at the closing with the proceeds from the reverse mortgage.

OUTLIVING THE REVERSE MORTGAGE

The loan does not become due as long as at least one of the homeowners lives in the home. It must be their primary residence, and they must keep the home by FHA requirements, which include maintaining the property and keeping the insurance and taxes current.

ESTATE INHERITANCE

In the event of death or the home ceases to be the primary residence for more than twelve months, the estate has the choice to repay the reverse mortgage or sell the home. If the equity in the home is higher than the balance of the loan, then the remaining equity belongs to the estate. The lender must take a loss and request reimbursement from the FHA if the sale of the home is not enough to pay off the reverse mortgage.

LOAN LIMITS

Four factors determine how much you will receive, they are:

- Age (the older, the better)
- Current interest rate
- Home's appraisal value
- Lending limits imposed by the Government

FEATURES OF A REVERSE MORTGAGE

- You always retain title to or ownership of your home.

- The older you are, the more money you receive.

- You have a choice of how you receive your funds.

MONEY DISTRIBUTION

With a reverse mortgage, you may receive the proceeds in several ways:

Lump Sum the total of all of the money at the closing.

Tenure as long as the property is where the homeowner lives, they may receive equal monthly payments.

Term for a fixed number of years, you may receive monthly payments.

Line of Credit until the line of credit is used up, you may draw any amount at any time. The portion of your line of credit not used, gains interest. You may use any combination of the above listed.

REVERSE MORTGAGE ADVANTAGES AND DISADVANTAGES

To determine whether a reverse mortgage is right for you, weigh the advantages against the disadvantages.

ADVANTAGES

You remain in your home with no mortgage payments. As long as you live in the home and adhere to the loan terms (taxes, insurance, and home maintenance) payment is not required.

- You can cover your expenses and have a supplement added to your fixed income.

- You have the option to choose how you use your equity.

- You do not have to pay additional income tax.

- You are not liable for any amount above your home's value.

- Your interest rates are comparable to home equity and traditional mortgage rates.

- You are required to undergo counseling so you can make an informed choice.

- You receive protection by government regulations from excessive fees.

- You can prepay and not attain penalties.

- The financing you receive is allowed to pay your upfront costs, so you do not, have to pay out of pocket.

DISADVANTAGES

- The upfront fees may be higher than other methods of financing.

- The equity left to your heirs may be reduced.

- The Reverse Mortgage may prevent you from getting need-based government assistance benefits.

- If the terms of the mortgage are violated, it may become due and payable in full.

- You cannot deduct interest accrued on taxes until the loan is due. You will not have future equity to liquidate.

FIVE MISCONCEPTIONS OF REVERSE MORTGAGES

1. **BANK/LENDER WILL TAKE YOUR HOME**

The banks make loans and earn interest. The lender adds a lien on the title so that they can get paid back the money borrowed.

2. **A REVERSE MORTGAGE CAN BE OUTLIVED**

If the homeowner moves out of the property for twelve consecutive months or dies, the reverse mortgage is due.

3. **THE HOME WILL NOT BE INHERITED BY THE ESTATE**

The estate inherits the home, but there is a lien on the title for any proceeds received, plus interest accrued.

4. **TAXES ARE PAID ON A REVERSE MORTGAGE**

Reverse Mortgage proceeds are exempt as income and, is not taxable. When repaid, the interest can be deductible. Talk to a tax consultant for more information.

5. **YOU CANNOT LOSE YOUR HOME WITH A REVERSE MORTGAGE**

To maintain your reverse mortgage, you **MUST** pay your property taxes (unless exempt), keep current homeowners insurance, and maintain your property.

APPLICATION STEPS

The application process for a reverse mortgage takes thirty (30) to forty-five (45) days from beginning to end and consists of five steps:

- Application
- Reverse Mortgage Counseling
- Appraisal
- Underwriting
- Closing

COST

FHA Mortgage Insurance, which guarantees that:

- The homeowner cannot outlive the reverse mortgage.

- The homeowner/heirs will not be liable if the loan balance exceeds the value of the home when sold.

- If the lender becomes financially distressed, FHA will take over the loan.

ORIGINATION

What the lender earns using an FHA formula. 2% of the property valued up to $200,000 and 1% if over $200,000, $6000 is the maximum they can charge.

TITLE

The homeowners legal ownership is guaranteed. Title fees are as follows:

- Title insurance (variable by property value and state)
- Title settlement
- Title search/examination
- Recording
- Courier/delivery
- Payoff (if you are paying off a mortgage)
- Notary
- Document preparation

APPRAISAL

The appraisal establishes the legal value of your home. An FHA-approved appraiser who follows specific guidelines, and provides more of the required documentation handles a reverse mortgage. The cost is usually in the range of $475 - $550 which is determined by the state involved.

ADDITIONAL COST

- Credit Report
- Flood Certificate
- Counseling
- Wire Costs

INTEREST

Interest is accrued just like a traditional loan. However, the homeowner does not make monthly payments to reduce the balance. The loan balance grows until the homeowner moves or passes away.

MARRIED COUPLES

Both individuals should be at least sixty-two (62) years of age. The calculation of money received is based on the income of the youngest person on the application. If one of the spouses is under the age of sixty-two (62), they are considered as an heir.

OVERVIEW

In my opinion, a reverse mortgage is an excellent option for seniors. I say this because, I have noticed that when seniors pass on, the next generation does not want to move back to the "old" neighborhood. They usually sell the property, or they lose the house for taxes.

The seniors can live in the comfort of their homes for the duration of their lives. If the heirs want the property, they simply have to pay the amount owed on the house.

I have given you a brief overview of the reverse mortgage process. If this is something you might be interested in, seek counseling through NCOA's (National Council on Aging) HUD-approved Reverse Mortgage Network at 800-510-0301.

I wanted to share this information with you, about Reverse Mortgages because my mother got one. At the time, she was eighty-seven years of age, and she used hers for home repairs and enhancements so she could enjoy the fruits of her labor. Then she had owned her home for fifty-two years.

Chapter 2

PREFERRED HOMEMAKER PROGRAM

The Preferred Homemaker Program assists seniors with staying in their homes. Those who benefit from these services are seniors whose doctors determine that their medical needs can be met at home. It is also, for those families who want to keep their loved ones home, and seniors who do not qualify for state or federal funding programs.

A Preferred Homemaker is a person selected by the senior (65+) to assist in such duties as:

- Light housekeeping
- Shopping
- Errands
- Teaching activities
- Meal preparation
- Laundry
- Money management
- Personal escort
- Personal care
- Bathing
- Grooming

A PREFERRED HOMEMAKER

- A well-known family member or friend who is liked, and trusted is paid by the state through a selected agency, twice a month

- Receives life insurance

- Has an opportunity to participate in a 401K plan

- Is given three days of training prior to employment and quarterly training after that

- Has a job as long as the senior remains in their home

The intention is to allow seniors (65+) the ability to stay in their homes and keep their independence by eliminating the need for them to do regular household tasks or run errands, etc.

Have the senior call 311 and ask for the Department of Aging (DOA) to request the services of a preferred homemaker. DOA will set up an appointment for a representative to interview the senior to determine how many hours per week a preferred homemaker would be authorized to work. After the interview, the senior will be given a list of certified agencies that will provide training for the selected homemaker.

PREFERRED HOMEMAKER QUALIFICATIONS

- Tuberculosis test (you pay)

- Background checks and fingerprinting (agency pays)

- No smoking or drinking on duty

I am my ninety-four-year-old mother's Preferred Homemaker. An entirely win-win situation occurs when this particular arrangement is in place. The senior wins, the homemaker wins, and the economy win. This program offers an excellent opportunity for trusted family members or friends to care for their loved ones with compensation.

Chapter 3

NETWORKING

Networking is an activity by which groups of like-minded businesspeople recognize, create, or act upon business opportunities. A business network is a type of social network whose reason for existing is to expand business activity.

NETWORKING TIPS

ALWAYS LOOK AT AND READ A PERSON'S BUSINESS CARD BEFORE PUTTING IT IN YOUR POCKET OR PURSE

In some Asian countries, it is considered an insult if you put a business card in your pocket or purse after someone gives it to you. Reading it in the presence of the person that gave it to you shows respect. On the practical side, having the person and the card together makes it possible to verify names, pronunciation and the business of the person you have just met. It is also a common courtesy.

SEND OR GIVE THANK YOU CARDS

Acknowledge referrals and leads that result in business. It makes you stand out from other contacts, and it keeps you in the recipient's mind in a positive manner.

DEVELOP A 30 SECOND ELEVATOR SPEECH

It should tell who you are, what you do, and who is a good lead or referral for you. You should have a tagline so people will remember you. When I am out networking, people always remember me by my tagline; it makes them laugh:

Good morning, I am Vivian Brazil, that's Brazil like the country, not like the nut. Shaklee, which has been in business helping millions of people since 1956, is my claim to fame. Enhanced health and safe environment, that's my game. I show you the advantages and benefits of using natural and green products and give you a satisfaction guarantee.

In the words of the late Reverend. Ike, "You can't lose, with this stuff I use."

A good lead or referral for me is anyone that wants to lose weight, relieve pain or stress, supplement their diet and create an environmentally safe home atmosphere. So, for life enhancement, come to Brazil, like the country.

STAND OUT

- Wear unique jewelry
- Wear bright colors
- Wear a unique hair color or style
- Smile, be friendly and helpful

*All of the above are conversation starters to get people talking to you.

DO NOT JUST GO OUT TO NETWORK NETWORK AS YOU GO OUT

Every place you go provides an opportunity to network. As you meet people and engage them in conversation, pay close attention to what they are saying. You will be able to determine if and how you will be able to provide a service, product or make referrals simply by listening to them.

ALWAYS READ

Constant reading keeps you informed, it gives you ideas and gives you something to talk about when meeting people. It also offers opportunities to help people, by sharing your knowledge and information.

FIND OUT WHAT OTHERS DO

When you first meet someone, make it a point to listen carefully to them before you speak. Ask at least one question before completing the conversation. It helps you to become quickly engaged in what they are saying and gets you connected. When you intentionally show interest in others, they reciprocate. If you know what others do, then you can either choose to use their services or refer them to others.

ALWAYS GET THE OTHER PERSON'S INFORMATION

Business cards are one of the most important marketing tools you can use. However, it may not be enough. A business card alone, will not serve the purpose of ensuring that people remember who you are. Make small talk and get them comfortable enough to give you their information. If they have a business card, make sure you exchange cards. If they do not have one, always get their name and telephone number.

The one who has the information is in control of making the follow-up call. If you just give out your card, you may never hear from them.

COMPLIMENT OTHERS

There is always something about the other person that you can compliment (i.e., hair, eyes, smile, voice, nails, shoes, or clothes). You make the other person feel good. You never know what others are dealing with at any given moment.

One day, I complimented a woman on her beautiful hair. She stopped, looked at me, and said that she was having a rough day and that I was the best thing that had happened to her that day.

NETWORKING VS ADVERTISING

Exchanging conversation, information, and business cards is networking. Getting related to people by finding out what matters to them adds a personal touch.

Randomly passing out business cards and flyers with no interaction is advertising. This activity could be considered cold and impersonal. However, there is an exception to every rule. You still want to get the information out. Passing out a large amount of flyer is a numbers game and the more people you reach, the better chance you have of them contacting you.

A friend of mine told me that he met the founder of Ace's Business Network A'fair (ABNA) by picking up a business card from the seat of a bus. He contacted him, became a member of the networking group and they developed a long standing relationship.

LAUGHTER

It makes people receptive
It is healing
It makes people feel good

SELL YOURSELF

People do business with people they know, like, and trust. Be a product of your product, no matter what it is, so that you can speak from experience.

IT IS NOT ONLY WHAT YOU KNOW, BUT WHO YOU KNOW, AND WHO KNOWS YOU

When you realize what is important to you in business, and you have definite goals, you need to start looking for those that can help you. These individuals should know who you are, what you do, and who is a good lead for you.

LEARN FROM YOUR FAILURES, BUT FOCUS ON YOUR SUCCESS

Allow failure to be your teacher. It shows you what did not work. When you focus on your success, and you are grateful, that gratitude opens the path for more success.

DO NOT MONOPOLIZE THE PERSON'S TIME

At networking events, be mindful that the objective is to leave with a name and phone number with the intention of talking later. Say a few words and move on allowing others the same opportunity.

KEEP YOUR WORD

When you say you are going to do something, do it. In networking relationships, mutual trust is critical. Trust gets destroyed when you do not follow through.

HAVE A FIRM HANDSHAKE

The benefits of a firm handshake include projecting power, confidence, and friendliness. These are imperative qualities to making a "good" impression when meeting someone for the first time.

GIVE

Share your time, knowledge, skills and suggestions to help others. Help causes and charities. If you have products, provide samples. When you give, you empower yourself to receive.

FOLLOW UP

In the follow-up call, you can build an instant rapport by using the simple acronym F.O.R.M: F stand for Family. Everyone loves talking about their family. O stands for Occupation, what they currently do for a living. R stands for Recreation when you listen to what people enjoy doing in their life makes them comfortable with you. M stands for Message, listening to what's important to them, allows you to sum up what they've said and helps you to develop a relationship so you can determine how you can be mutually beneficial. This call is to establish a partnership by either becoming a customer or referring customers.

SPEED NETWORKING

Speed networking is a meeting format designed to accelerate business contacts, generally with a bell. Primarily, the practice involves multiple people that gather to exchange information. Participants greet each other in a series of brief exchanges during a set period. During an interaction, attendees share their professional backgrounds and business goals. Networkers are generally seeking exposure to new markets and/or to expand their pool of vendors.

TYPES OF SPEED NETWORKING

There are three types of speed networking:

Round Robin

In the round robin model of Speed Networking attendees meet each other sequentially.

Station-Based

In the station-based model of Speed Networking, attendees meet each other individually based on a predetermined assignment.

Group-Based

In the group-based model of Speed Networking attendees do not meet individually. Instead, they are assigned to a sequence of tables.

Goals that business professionals commonly have in mind when networking are:

- To exchange qualified business leads
- To get top quality service
- To get "out-of-reach" customers
- To learn business development skills
- To have the potential to increase revenues
- To establish long-term friendships

Networking is essential for strong business development. We need other people to buy from us, sell to us, and brainstorm with us to progress in our field. To have people do these things for us, we must be willing to give of ourselves in return.

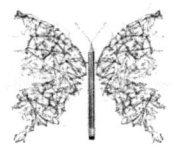

Chapter 4

VOLUNTEERING

There are all types of organizations that can benefit from volunteers. These establishments include community organizations, churches, homeless shelters, boy's and girl's clubs, schools, people in recovery, ex-offenders, after school programs, theaters, museums, libraries and senior centers.

When you volunteer, you bring with you, experience, skills, knowledge, and ideas to help the organization. When considering an organization, the key is to find one with a cause that matches your belief system. Then find a position within the organization that you enjoy and are capable of doing. Make sure that your commitment matches the organization's needs.

Matching your skills and interest is the best way to volunteer. Is there something specific that you would like to do? Are you interested in helping to better the neighborhood where you live? Do you want to meet people who are different from you? Do you want to do something meaningful with your spare time or see a different way of life? What better way is there to visit and experience new places? Volunteering allows you to utilize and discover talents that you are good at and enjoy.

In determining the right volunteer opportunity you should decide:

- Is there a particular cause that is important to you?
- Do you want to work with people or alone?
- How much responsibility are you willing to take on?
- What skills do you have to bring to the organization?
- Do you want a visible role or would you rather work behind the scenes?

BENEFITS OF BEING A VOLUNTEER

You have an opportunity to make a difference in your community. Volunteering is about helping people and impacting others' wellbeing. There is no better way to give back to society than to offer some of the benefits that humanity has given you while helping out in your own neighborhood.

You have the opportunity to help. Volunteering allows you to bring your experiences and skills for the betterment of others.

You have the opportunity to learn. Volunteering gives you a chance to learn about the various aspects of the organization.

You have the possibility of sharpening your skills. Volunteering allows you to use your various skills, therefore enhancing them. It gives you a sense of achievement. Volunteering makes you feel good about helping others. It gives you a sense of pride and identity and keeps you from becoming depressed.

You get an occasion to meet many new people. Volunteering brings a diverse range of individuals from all walks of life, new industries, and different environments.

You get new life experiences. Through hands-on work, you will experience the real world.

Volunteering boosts your self-confidence. Doing noble deeds for others provides a sense of accomplishment, and as you feel better about yourself, you will view your life and future goals more positively.

Volunteering helps you make new friends and contacts. As a volunteer, your network expands, bringing together people with mutual interests, resources, and activities. Social isolation is a deadly factor in depression and volunteering helps to ward off such feelings. Volunteering also puts you in regular contact with others, which is vital to the establishment of a support system to help protect you from stress when you are going through life altering challenges.

Volunteering has many fringe benefits such as:

- Meals
- Invitations to various affairs
- Token gifts
- Inside information
- Memorabilia in the form of autographed letters, certificates and tokens from people who may in the future be or become famous

(See Exhibits 3, 4 & 5 in Chapter 10)

An amazing thing about volunteering is that it has healing power. The power of the mind to influence the body is beyond question. Helping others gives you a positive mental attitude that will trigger changes in the body that promote healing and health.

During my lifetime, I volunteered for many committees within the postal service and worked on behalf of political candidates, including President Obama. I also volunteered at Clara's House, a shelter for homeless women and children, and for The International Stevenson Foundation, an organization that helps ex-offenders and people in substance abuse recovery. *(See Exhibits in Chapter 10)*.

Mom volunteered at her church in the healing ministry. She aided the sick and shut in by sending out get well cards. We all love to find a colorful hand-addressed envelope from our place of worship when we are dealing with an illness. It gives us a sense of support that shows care and concern for our well-being. She also shared her gifts and talents with those who were dealing with unfortunate challenges by serving in the food pantry ministry.

Volunteering allows you to aid society through organizations and reap the "feel good" benefit of helping those less fortunate. You become part of a creative force for the betterment of mankind and the organization by working together with other like-minded individuals. Lifelong friendships are often developed when volunteers work together to help a good cause. When you volunteer, you bless and are blessed.

VOLUNTEER

V – VALUE
A volunteer adds value to others
with their knowledge skills and abilities.

O – OFFERS
A volunteer offers their talents and skills
for the betterment of mankind.

L – LOVE
A volunteer shows love for mankind by
performing a variety of tasks for organizations.

U – UNSELFISH
A volunteer is unselfish
in sharing their knowledge, talents, and skills.

N – NURTURES
A volunteer nurtures others by demonstrating and developing
numerous skills and abilities.

T – TEACHES
A volunteer teaches and instructs
activities for the organization.

E – EXPERTISE
A volunteer brings their expertise to the organization.

E – EMPATHY
A volunteer shows compassion in dealing with others.

R – REGARD
A volunteer has regard for the feelings of others.

A volunteer is a person that donates time, knowledge and skills to an organization for the betterment of their cause. Those who regularly volunteer and help others, normally have a healthier, more positive outlook on life.

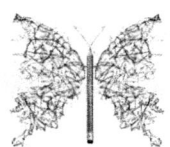

Chapter 5

ADVICE AND SUGGESTIONS
WRITE YOUR OWN OBITUARY

I recommend that you write your own obituary, because no one knows you, your life, and your accomplishments better than you.

- It takes some of the pressure off of your loved ones
- You can pick your favorite scriptures
- You can select your favorite songs

I came up with this idea when, one of my co-workers died. She had written her own obituary. It started out with,
"To those I love and to those that love me."
That really made an impression on me.

Another co-worker died, but his family had nothing about his major life accomplishments documented in his obituary. The fact that he had worked on his job for thirty-five years was a huge achievement that did not get mentioned.

One day out of the blue, my mother asked me to write her obituary. She gave me a list of things that were important to her to include in the document. Listed were the things she wanted her family and friends to know. On my own, I would never have thought to include many of those things. Now, our family is better prepared when the time comes.

IDENTIFY KEY PEOPLE IN YOUR PHONE BOOK

List the key people that you want your family to notify when you pass on. In your personal phone book, put an asterisk (*) by their names to indicate your intentions for your family to contact them. Be sure to let them know that you want them to inform those in your circle of friends and associates of your transition. If you belong to various clubs, groups, or organizations, indicate the people that you expect to help in getting the word out.

SPEND QUALITY TIME WITH YOUR GRANDCHILDREN

After I had retired, I started *"A day out with Grandma"* with my two grandsons. Our day was the first Tuesday of every month. I would take them out to do whatever they wanted. Sometimes we would go to movies, museums, amusement parks, shopping malls, or to an arcade.

We would always end up at a fast food or dine-in restaurant. I started giving them their own money to spend because one day when we were at the arcade; they kept asking me to get more tokens for the games. I gave each of them a twenty dollar bill and told them that they would handle everything including their food. That day they only bought a dollar worth of tokens.

Lesson: *Children will spend your money freely and hold on to theirs.*

I feel that this special day taught my grandsons dependability (they could always count on Grandma). Cultivating this personal time with my grandson's exposed them to many different life experiences such as how to act in public, responsibility with their money and it gave them cherished memories. Those special occasions were also a great bonding experience that allowed me to pass down my legacy to them.

A friend of mine graciously shared with me how she bonds with her grandchildren, who live out of town. She said, every month, she sent them a Christmas card with money.

When you bond with your grandchildren, you are creating memories for them. You are also planting seeds for your future because what you give, you will receive. My grandchildren have started to reciprocate. Now that they have grown up, I get taken out by them.

TEACH YOUR CHILDREN/GRANDCHILDREN THE GOLDEN RULE

When my grandsons were too young to sit in the front seat of the car, I would have them sit in the back seat and buckle up. I would always ask them, "What's the golden rule?" They would tell me, "Do unto others as you would have them do unto you." Then I would ask them, "What does it mean?" They would tell me, "Don't do anything to anybody that you wouldn't want done to you."

When I visited my grandson, Mario's Facebook page, I saw that he chose the golden rule as his favorite quote. Can you imagine how good I felt seeing that?

TEACH YOUR CHILDREN/GRANDCHILDREN THEIR NAMES AND PARENTS NAMES

I saw on the local news that a child approximately 3 or 4 years-old was found running down the street alone at night. They kept flashing the child's picture and asking if anyone knew him. This particular child only knew his nickname.

It is important that children be taught their name and their parents' names as soon as they begin to talk. It is important to take intentional time with children to assure that they are pronouncing the names correctly. When the authorities are not sure of what the child is saying errors can still occur.

SCRAPE OR BRUSH YOUR TONGUE DAILY

After you brush your teeth and before you rinse your mouth, scrape or brush your tongue. It is surprising what comes off. Performing this technique, helps make and keep your breath fresh.

VISIT THE SICK AND SHUT-IN

Visiting the sick and shut-in is a powerful experience. The people that you visit, sometimes end up cheering you up. Your visit could be an encouragement and inspiration to someone who's having a difficult time. It turns out that visiting the sick and shut-in is healing to your soul as well as the person you are visiting.

BITS OF WISDOM TO LIVE BY

1. I love you because of who I am when I am with you, not because of who you are.

2. The man or woman who is worth your tears, will not make you cry.

3. Because a person does not love you the way you want them to, does not mean that they do not love you with all they have.

4. A real friend is someone who reaches for your hand, but touches your heart.

5. Smile because it happened, don't cry because it's over.

6. The best things happen when you least expect them, so relax and go with the flow.

7. When you are sad, never frown because you never know who is falling in love with your smile.

8. Know and love yourself before you expect it of someone else.

9. We must meet a few of the wrong people in our lifetime, so we will know how to be grateful when we meet the right person.

10. Believe that everything happens for a reason for your highest good.

11. Aspire to inspire before you expire.

LIFE ETHICS

BELIEVE – before you pray
LISTEN – before you speak
EARN – before you spend
THINK – before you write
TRY – before you quit
LIVE – before you die

BABY, SUCK A THUMB

A dear friend shared this amazing tip with me to prevent getting lipstick on your teeth. After you have applied your lipstick, stick your thumb in your mouth and take it out. Notice the ring left on your thumb. You might want to share this tip with anyone you see with lipstick on their teeth.

WHAT WILL YOUR LEGACY BE?

These were the words of Dr. Margaret Burroughs, who was my aunt by marriage. "Stop and think, what are you leaving for your children and grandchildren?" What words of wisdom, funny memories, lessons taught, businesses started, or fortunes left, will your loved ones have from you?

Chapter 6

REFLECTIONS

With the help of my mother, Ruth Webb, in raising my daughter, Yvonne, I was able to finish high school and get my diploma, as a teenage mother. Mom, who was raising her children and volunteering for her churches, also worked and retired from Chicago Allis Rubber. She received a birthday card on her 90th birthday from President Barack Obama. *(See Exhibit 21)*

My sister, Sherice, is ten months older than my daughter, so we raised them as sisters. Sherice has two sons, Terrence Ryan and Kenton Demario. They reside in the state of Oklahoma. My brother, Wilbert (deceased), was a Vietnam Veteran and worked for the Postal Service until his demise. My father, Willie Webb (deceased), worked for thirty-five years at Revere Copper and Brass before retiring.

Yvonne, my one, and only child, always volunteered me for all of her class trips. She was a sweet child and never caused any problems. When she was about fifteen years old, she brought me an article about Barbizon Modeling School and said that she would like to take some classes there. I enrolled her, and she attended the classes for a couple of years. She also entered the Miss Black Teenage World of Illinois. She won two awards. One was "Top Teen" for the most ads, the most patrons, and the other was "Miss Congeniality." Out of thirteen girls, she was voted to have the most pleasing personality.

Once she turned seventeen, my daughter Yvonne continued receiving courses at Barbizon Modeling School in Chicago, on Michigan Ave. She later joined Innovations Modeling Agency.

In 1982, she was crowned "Ms. Innovations" in the agency's pageant. She showcased her talents as a hair model in a featured article for Elanceé Magazine.

Yvonne has had employment with Northern Trust Bank for over thirty-five years.

Paul, my oldest grandson, has always been an exceptional child, academically. He was one of two children from Beasley Academy, whose poems were selected to be published. At the age of twelve, his poetry appeared in the *Chicago's Hands on Stanzas* 2003-2004 *Anthology of Poetry*, *(see Exhibit 1, page 102)*.

In high school, he was one of the top twenty-five students in his graduating class. He was also a PSA scholar and was exempt from taking final exams to graduate. He received a scholarship to the University of Illinois in Champaign-Urbana. He wrote an "A" Essay about his grandmother.

My Grandmother
by
Paul Jordan

My grandmother is a very unique and wonderful person. Her story begins on August 25, 1946, which was the first day she experienced the outside world. She had a normal birth like most children so her birth was ordinary. She had a pretty normal childhood, at least from what I was told anyway. Her life changed dramatically, though, as a teenager. At the age of sixteen, a little more than a month from her birthday she had a baby and birthed my mother.

After that, the rest of her teenage years went from having fun to work and raising a child. Back then it was extremely difficult to raise a child, but she managed to do it and still enjoyed her life. I can still remember, though, her telling me everything she had to go through and it wasn't easy for her, especially since she had to do it mostly on her own. She got some help from my great-grandmother, but not much because my great-grandmother is a very stern person and wanted my grandmother to learn how to take care of herself and her child, especially since she made the mistake. My grandmother always tells me she never regretted what she did because if she didn't she wouldn't have my brother and me.

As my grandmother got older she was very adventurous. She also is a very affectionate, generous, and loving grandmother. She really enjoys traveling and has been to many different places. She also collects as many souvenirs as she can so she can share the stories of her travels and show the interesting things she gets. She also took up many hobbies like reading, gambling, exercising, stepping and bowling. She has a vast collection of books, which most are about bettering one's self, ways of becoming successful, or inspirational books. Some of her favorites are Rich Dad, Poor Dad and Young Lions.

She is a great gambler and loves to play card games. She has taught my brother and me a great deal of poker games and just games to have fun. My grandmother, unlike most adults around her age is very active and does things like she was still in her twenties or early thirties. She feels and acts younger than her actual age and is in good shape for a woman her age. My grandmother, like most older people enjoys going out to a stepper's club. She does this pretty much every Friday and that's one of her ways to staying active and healthy. She also is an excellent bowler. She is part of a bowling team and they compete in tournaments from time to time. I have never even come close to beating her and I never expect to either.

We also have this agreement between me, her and my brother, which started about five or six years ago. The agreement is every first Tuesday of every month is our day to spend time together and we do whatever we can think of to have fun together.

The most surprising thing to me about this agreement was that it was all her idea. There is a catch though, when my brother and me get older and have careers, she wants us to take her out every first Tuesday of every month and take her out to do what she wants.

She also wants us to buy her a purple Jaguar and a new house. My grandmother has a unique fashion style and it is very unique. She loves the color purple and has a lot of clothes, shoes, jewelry, sunglasses, and anything else that looks good in purple. Moreover she has tons of stuff anyway. She actually is kind of a "pack rat."

She is also an entrepreneur and has a home based business. It is called Shaklee and the types of products she sells are all natural health and environmentally friendly consumer products. My mother has even purchased some of these products and they are really helpful and healthy. She is only sixty-three years of age and has accomplished and experienced so much in her life and still has more to come. Oh, and I forgot to mention that she retired from the post office after 35 years of service. All in all, my grandmother is a very unique, affectionate, generous, and a loving person and I love her.

Mario, my youngest grandson, always excelled in athletics. He has earned numerous medals in cross country track and field, tumbling, and gymnastics (Exhibitt 2, Chapter 10). Although he was outstanding in sports, the school said he was ADHD, and he failed the third grade. They recommended medication for him, but my daughter would not allow them to medicate him.

When the family moved, his school was changed, and he began to excel. They promoted him to his right grade after he enrolled in the 8th-grade transitioning program at his junior high school. He ended his high school academic year with good grades and was awarded a scholarship to Ashford University in Iowa.

Reverend Dr. Johnnie Coleman was my spiritual teacher. I began attending Christ Universal Temple in 1996 as a "Friend." Rev. Coleman wrote one of the best sets of easy-to-read books that I have ever read. The eight-volume set is titled *"It Works If You Work It."*

When I volunteered at Clara's House, a women's homeless shelter, I read them to the ladies and their children. Rev. Coleman taught me to stand on my own "spiritual feet."

Bishop Carlton Pearson, my current pastor, and spiritual leader is helping me to recognize what I believe about myself. His counseling allows me to understand why I feel the way I do, and how those beliefs add to or subtract from the quality of my life. He also teaches and reminds me of my personal powerful and often forgotten divinity.

Chapter 7

55 THINGS I HAVE LEARNED

1. Put God before everything
2. Always follow the golden rule
3. Always be your best
4. Stay positive
5. Continue learning
6. Don't quit
7. Watch your:
   - Words
   - Thoughts
   - Feelings
   - Actions
   - Reactions
8. Reading expands your thoughts and vision
9. Know who and whose you are

10. Find a mentor and be a mentor
11. Seek others for assistance
12. Consciousness is the key
13. Follow Christ
14. Share your knowledge
15. Be specific
16. Write the vision
17. Help others to recognize their greatness
18. Welcome change
19. Know when to quit
20. Laugh often
21. When you teach, it enhances your skills
22. Stand firm on your principles
23. Set goals
24. Dancing is excellent exercise
25. Love yourself so you can love others
26. We were born to prosper
27. Choose wisely
28. Always look your best

29. Take care of your business
30. Use mistakes as learning experiences
31. Forgive yourself so you can forgive others
32. Understand the value of tithing
33. Always show gratitude to God, and others
34. Experience new and different things
35. Like attracts like, so be what you want
36. Find out your purpose (ask God)
37. Today is the first day of the rest of your life
38. Exercise regularly
39. Start the way you intend to finish
40. Things don't have to be expensive to be valuable
41. Be flexible
42. Do what makes you feel good
43. Take time for yourself
44. Be nice
45. Reading is fundamental
46. Don't shed tears over anything that can't cry for you

47. Learn how to say no to things you don't want to do
48. It's good to take a nap
49. Take vitamins
50. Collect something
51. Smile
52. Have fun life is short
53. Enjoy your life
54. Always give people more than they expect

and finally

55. Pray and go with the flow

HANDY HELPFUL TIPS

To remove blood stains from clothes, just pour a little hydrogen peroxide on a cloth and wipe the stain until it's gone.

To remove crayon marks from a wall, use a damp cloth dipped in baking soda.

Ever seal an envelope and realize that you forgot something? Place the envelope in the freezer for a few hours, and slide a knife under the flap, and then reseal the envelope.

Empty toilet paper rolls can be used to store extension and appliance cords. You can even write what device it belongs to, right on the roll as a label.

When washing windows, use vertical strokes on the outside and horizontal strokes on the inside. This way you can tell which side has the streaks.

- Use straight vinegar for really clean outside windows.
- Don't wash windows on a sunny day. They will dry too fast and probably streak.

To create a lovely light scent in your rooms, spray a bit of perfume on the light bulb. When you turn on the lights, you will smell the scent as the bulb heats.

To clean salt from your leather boots or shoes, mix

one tablespoon of white vinegar in one cup of cold water. Use a clean, soft cloth dipped in the solution and squeeze out the excess. Wipe the salt spots until gone and let dry. Place the leftover solution in a container with a top and use again.

To clean stainless-steel surfaces, sprinkle with baking soda and wipe with a damp sponge.

To remove wine stains from carpeting, sprinkle baking soda and dab with a damp cloth or sponge. Continue the procedure until the stain is gone.

To keep your clothes smelling fresh place fabric softener sheets in drawers and linen cabinets.

When you get a splinter, put scotch tape over the splinter and pull it out. Scotch tape removes most splinters painlessly and easy.

To stop the itch from a mosquito bite, apply soap to the area, and you will experience instant relief.

Add a pinch of sugar when boiling corn on the cob to help bring out the natural sweetness.

Celery will keep for weeks in the refrigerator if you put it in aluminum foil.

To remove burnt food from your skillet easily, add enough water to cover the bottom of the pan, two drops of dish liquid and bring to a boil on top of the stove.

Carry your personalized address labels in your wallet. You can use them for:

- Bank deposit slips
- Church offerings
- Anywhere there is a need for you to write your name and address

To clean and freshen your refrigerator, sprinkle equal amounts of baking soda and salt on a damp cloth or sponge and wipe the surfaces.

To relieve the itch of bug bites and bee stings, mix equal parts of salt and baking soda then brush onto the area affected.

To clean your gold and silver jewelry, mix three parts baking soda to 1 part water. Gently rub, then rinse. Shine with a soft cloth.

Got an attractive bottle you would like to keep? To smoothly remove the label, soak it in a sink of hot water and add a couple of drops of dish detergent.

FAINTING

Are you feeling faint? To keep from losing consciousness, sit in the nearest chair, lean forward, and put your head between your knees. Your brain will receive a fresh supply of blood.

TO HELP YOU REMEMBER

To help you remember where you have put things, speak the location out loud as you store them.

HOW TO RECEIVE A GREETING CARD FROM THE PRESIDENT

- You must be a U. S. Citizen
- You must provide the name, address and date of birth or anniversary of the person to whom the letter should be sent. If you are requesting a letter for someone else, include your name and address also.
- For a baby's birth, you must submit a request within the first year of their birth. The request must come after the baby is born.
- The birthday card request must be for someone turning 80 or older or turning 70 if it's for a veteran.
- Must be for the 50th Anniversary or greater.

A response takes about six weeks, so plan accordingly. Send or fax the request to:

>The White House
>Attn: Greetings Office
>Washington, DC 20502-0039
>Fax No. (202) 395-1232

DID YOU KNOW

Did you know that when you reach the age of 65 if you enroll in Medicare Part B you can select Humana Gold HMO for no additional charge, including free medication? Also, you become a member of Silver Sneakers, where you may go to various health clubs for no extra charge.

WORDS WITH NO RHYME

There are no words in the English language that rhyme with purple, silver, month, or orange.

THE QUICK BROWN FOX

"The quick brown fox jumps over the lazy dog" uses every letter of the alphabet.

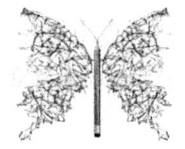

Chapter 8

LAUGHTER FOR THE SOUL

THE SCIENTIST

God is sitting in heaven when a scientist prays to Him.

Scientist: "God, we don't need you anymore. Science has finally figured out a way to create life out of nothing – in other words; we can now do what did in the beginning."

GOD: "Oh, is that so? Tell me."

Scientist: "Well, we can take dirt and form it into the likeness of you and then breathe life into it thus creating man."

GOD: "Well, that's very interesting…show me."

So, the scientist bends down to the earth and starts to mold the soil into a shape of a man.

GOD: "No, no, no..." Interrupts God. "MAKE YOUR OWN DIRT."

AGING

Three seniors were sitting on a park bench.

"Sixty is the worst age to be," said the sixty-year-old man.

"You always feel like you have to pee and most of the time you stand there and nothing comes out."

"That's nothing," said the seventy-year-old. "When you're seventy, you don't have a bowel movement anymore. You eat bran, take laxatives and sit on the toilet all day and nothing comes out."

"Actually," said the eighty-year-old, "Eighty is the worst age of all."

"Do you have trouble peeing too," asked the sixty-year- old.

"No, I pee every morning at six o'clock like a racehorse, no problem at all." Said the eighty-year-old."

"So, do you have a problem with your bowel movement?" Asked the seventy-year-old.

"No, I have one every morning at 6:30" replied the eighty-year-old.

Exasperated, the sixty-year-old said, "You pee every morning at 6:00 and crap every morning at 6:30? So what's so bad about being eighty?"

"I don't wake up until seven o'clock." Replied the eighty-year-old.

BABY DADDY?

A man goes into the grocery store and notices an attractive woman waving at him. "Hello," she says.

But, he's puzzled because he can't place her. So he asked, "Do you know me?"

She says, "I think you're the father of one of my kids."

The man thinks back to the only time he was unfaithful to his wife and says, "Oh my God, are you the stripper from my bachelor party? The one I made love to on the pool table with all my buddies watching while your partner whipped my butt with wet celery?"

She looks calmly into his eyes and says, "No. I am your son's teacher."

SOMETIMES A WOMAN JUST HAS TO TRUST HER HUSBAND

Coming in late one night, a wife quietly opens her bedroom door. From under the blanket, she sees four legs instead of two. She grabs a baseball bat and starts hitting the blanket as hard as she could. When she finishes, she goes to have a drink in the kitchen. As she enters, she sees her husband sitting at the table reading the newspaper.

"Hi Dear," he says, "Your parents came to visit us, so I let them stay in our bedroom. Did you say hello?"

DRIVING SENIOR

As an elderly man was driving down the expressway, his car phone rang. When he answered it, his wife was on the line.

"Jim, I just heard on the news that there is a car going the wrong way on Interstate 66. Please be careful!" She said.

"Heck," said Jim, "It's not just one car. It's hundreds of them."

REMEMBERED ROMANCE

An elderly couple was lying in bed. The husband was falling asleep, but his wife was in a talkative and romantic mood.

"You used to hold my hand during our courtship." She said.

He reached across the bed and held her hand for a second and then tried to go back to sleep.

A minute later, the wife said, "Then you used to kiss me."

A little irritated, he leaned over and gave her a kiss on the cheek and settled back down to get some sleep.

Thirty seconds later the wife said, "Then you use to bite my neck."

Totally irritated, the husband throws off the bed covers and gets out of bed.

"Where are you going?" The wife asked.

"To get my teeth!" He replied.

THE GIFT

It was the last day of school, and all of the children in the kindergarten class brought presents for the teacher. The florist's son gave the teacher a gift. She shook it and held it up.

"I bet I know what it is – it's some flowers." She said.

"Right!" Shouted the boy.

Next the candy store owner's daughter gave her gift. She held it up and shook it.

"I bet I know what it is. It's a box of candy." She said.

"That's right," shouted, the little girl.

The next gift was from the liquor store owner's son. The teacher held it up and noticed that it was leaking. She touched a drop and tasted it.

"Is it wine?" She asked.

"No." Replied the little boy.

The teacher puts another drop to her tongue.

"Is it champagne?" She asked.

"No," the boy answered.

"I give up," said the teacher. "What is it?"

"It's a puppy" replied the little boy.

RETIREMENT CENTER

Eighty-five-year-old Alma runs into the recreation room at the retirement home. She raises her clenched fist in the air.

"Anyone who can guess what I am holding in my

hand can have sex with me tonight." She shouts.

An old man in the back of the room, responded, "It's an Elephant?"

Alma thinks for a few seconds and says, "Close enough."

GOING FOR A DRIVE

Two elderly women were out driving in a big car. Neither could barely see over the dashboard. As they were driving along, they came to an intersection. The stoplight was red, but they went through it. Mary, who was in the passenger's seat, thought to herself, Wow, I must be losing it. I could have sworn that we just went through that red light. In a few minutes, they came to another red light. They went right through that one too. Mary was really concerned that she was losing it and was getting nervous. At the next intersection, the light was red, and again they went through it. She turned to the other woman.

"Jean, did you know that you just ran through three red lights in a row? You could have killed us both!" She nervously said.

Jean turned to Mary and said, "Oh! Am I driving?"

I CAN HEAR OK

Three old gents, all with hearing loss, were golfing one breezy March day.

"Windy, isn't it?" Said the first gent to the other.

"No," said the second man, "It's Thursday."
The third man chimed in, "So am I. Let's have a bottle of beer."

HYPNOTIZED

At the Senior Citizen's Center, it was entertainment night. After the community sing-along led by Jan, the piano player, it was time for Charles the Hypnotist. Charles told the audience that he was going to put them in a trance.

"All of us?" A voice from the audience asked.

"Yes, all of you at the same time," said Charles.

The audience was silent as Charles carefully withdrew a beautiful antique gold pocket watch and chain from his suit jacket. Holding the beautiful watch high for all to see, he said, "I want you to keep looking at the watch. It's a very valuable watch that has been in my family for five generations."

He began to swing the watch gently back and forth while quietly saying:

"Watch the watch - Watch the watch - Watch the watch."

The audience was mesmerized as the watch swayed back and forth. The lights twinkled as they reflect from its gleaming surface. One hundred pairs of eyes followed the movement of the gently swaying watch.

All of a sudden, the chain broke. The beautiful watch fell and shattered into pieces on the stage floor

"SHIT!" Charles yelled.

It took three days to clean the Senior Citizens Center, Charles was never invited to entertain there again.

IT'S SUPER SEX

An old woman was walking up and down the halls of the nursing home. As she strolled, she would throw up her nightgown and say, "Super sex? Super sex?" She walked up to an old gent in a wheelchair and flipped up the hem of her gown and said, "Super sex?"

The old gent quietly sat there for a minute and finally answered, "I'll take the soup."

THE BATHTUB TEST

We should take a hard look at ourselves sometimes. This story should get us started. A man once asked the director of a mental asylum what standard they used to determine whether a patient should be institutionalized.

"Well, we fill up a bathtub, then we offer a teaspoon, a teacup, and a bucket to the patient and ask him or her to empty the bathtub," said the director.

"I understand," said the man. "A normal person would use the bucket because it's bigger than the spoon or the teacup."

"No," said the director, "a normal person would pull the plug. Do you want a bed near the window?"

DADDY'S GOING TO EAT YOUR FINGERS

As the father was packing for a business trip, his three-year-old daughter was playing on the bed. She suddenly said, "Daddy, look at this" and stuck out two of her fingers.

In an effort to entertain her, he reached out and stuck

her fingers in his mouth and said, "Daddy's going to eat your fingers!"

He pretended to eat them before rushing out of the room. When he returned, his daughter was standing on the bed staring at her fingers with a devastated look on her face.

He said, "What's wrong, sweetheart?"

"What happened to my booger?" Asked the little girl.

ANNIVERSARY

John was in big trouble. He forgot his wedding anniversary. His wife was furious.

"Tomorrow morning, I expect to find a gift in the driveway that goes from 0 to 200 in less than six seconds. AND, IT BETTER BE THERE," the wife announced.

The next morning John got up early and left for work. When his wife woke up, she looked out of the window and sure enough, there was a wrapped gift box in the middle of the driveway. Puzzled, John's wife put on her robe and went out to the driveway and got the package. When she opened it, she found a brand new shiny bathroom scale. John has been missing since Saturday.

DAD AT THE MALL

John took his ninety-year-old dad to the mall one day to buy him a pair of shoes. They decided to stop at the food court for something to eat. John noticed that his dad kept watching a teenager sitting next to him. The teenager had green, yellow, red, orange, and blue spiked hair. John's father kept looking at the youth. Every time the teenager looked up, he found John's dad staring at him. The teen finally had had enough.

"What's the matter old man, haven't you ever done anything wild in your life?" The teenager asked sarcastically.

John, knowing his dad would have a good response, quickly swallowed his food so he wouldn't choke.

The old man in classic style did not bat an eye and replied, "I Got drunk once and had sex with a peacock and was just wondering if you were my son."

TEACHER

The children had their pictures taken, and the teacher was trying to convince them to purchase a group photo.

"Just think," said the teacher, "twenty years from now, it will be nice to look at the picture and say, there's Michael, he's a doctor. Or there's Mary, she's a lawyer."

A small voice rang out from the back of the class.

"And there's the teacher. She's dead," shouted Johnny.

THE AIRPLANE RIDE

A man and woman were on an airplane seated side by side. The woman sneezed, took out a tissue, gently wiped her nose, and visibly shook for 6 to 10 seconds. The man, looked at her, then went back to reading. A few minutes later the woman sneezed again, took another tissue, wiped her nose, and then shook a little more violently. He assumed that the woman might have a cold, but he was curious about the shaking. Again, the woman sneezed, took a tissue, wiped her nose, and her body shook even more. The man's curiosity got the best of him.

"Are you OK?" Asked the man.

The woman answers, "I'm sorry for disturbing you. I have a rare medical condition. Whenever I sneeze, I have an orgasm."

The man, now embarrassed, but still curious said, "I have never heard of that condition before. Are you taking anything for it?"

"Yes," replied the woman, "I'm taking pepper."

FRIENDS

Carol and Donna, had been friends for several decades. Throughout the years, they had shared many adventures and activities. Now their activities had been limited to a few times a month.

One day while playing cards, Carol looked at Donna and said, "Now, don't get mad at me, but I can't for the life of me remember your name. Please tell me what it is."

Donna just glared at her for at least a minute and said, "How soon do you need to know?"

WALMART GREETERS

John and Joe, two elderly Walmart greeters, were sitting on a bench at break time. Joe said to John, "I'm eighty-five years old, and I have a lot of aches and pains. I know that you are about my age. How do you feel?"

John said, "I feel like a newborn baby."

Shocked by John's response, Joe replied,

"Oh really, a newborn baby?"

"Yup," grinned John, "no teeth, no hair, and I think I just wet my pants."

GROWTH

When Jan was six months pregnant, with her third child, her three-year-old daughter, Susan came into the room as she was getting ready to take a shower.

"Mommy you're getting fat," Susan said.

"Honey, remember that Mommy has a baby growing in her tummy," replied the mother.

I know about the baby growing in your tummy, remarked Susan. "What's growing in your butt?"

LIFESAVERS

A college professor was testing the senses of 2nd graders using a bowl of Lifesavers. After giving the same kind of lifesaver to all the children one at a time. He asked them to identify the candy by color and flavor.

"Orange... orange" "Green... lime" "Yellow... lemon" "Red... cherry," the children called out in unison.

Then the professor gave them all Honey Lifesavers. After they ate them, no one could associate the taste.

The professor then said, "I'll give you a clue. It is what your mother may call your father."

One little girl looked up in horror and yelled, "Spit them out! They're assholes!"

WOMAN ORGANIZED

Two women, Debbie, and Darlene met for the first time since they graduated from high school. Debbie said to Darlene, "You were the organized one in school. Did you manage to live a well-planned life?"

"Yes," said Darlene to her friend.

"My first husband was a millionaire, my second husband was an actor, my third husband was a preacher, and now I'm married to an undertaker."

Debbie asked, "What do all of those marriages have to do with a well-planned life?"

"One for the money, two for the show, three to get ready, and four to go." Shouted Darlene.

HOSPITAL NUNS

John suffered a severe heart attack and had to have bypass surgery. He woke up and found himself in a Catholic hospital in the care of nuns. After asking how he was going to pay the bill and finding out that he had no health insurance or money in the bank, a nun asked if he had a relative that could help him out.

"I just have a spinster sister who is a nun." Said John.

The nun, visibly disturbed by the comment said, "Nuns are not spinsters! Nuns are married to God."

"Well, in that case," replied John, "send my bill to my brother-in-law."

FAITH

Two nuns ran out of gas on the highway and flagged a truck down to get some help. The truck driver was willing to help them but didn't have anything to put the gas in and carry it. One of the nuns said, "It's okay. We have our own container. We are just returning from a nursing assignment, and there is a bedpan in our car."

The truck driver siphoned some gas into the bedpan and went on his way. As the nuns slowly poured the gas into the tank of their car to avoid spilling any, a passing motorist slowed down to see what the women were doing.

"Christ!" He said to his companion.
"That's what I call faith."

RED BICYCLE

Johnny, who was a little, bad boy, asked his mother for a red bicycle for his birthday. His mother told him to write a letter to God, and tell him why he deserved to get a bike. So, little Johnny's letter went like this—

"Dear God, I was a good boy last year, please give me a red bicycle for my birthday."

After reading the letter, he realized that indeed, he had not been a good boy; so he tore up the letter and wrote another one.

"Dear God, I am going to be a good boy for the next year—please give me a red bicycle for my birthday."

After he thought about it, realizing that he had such a difficult time being good, he also tore up that letter. When he went to Sunday morning mass, he saw a statue of the

Virgin Mary and stole it. After returning home, he wrote another letter:

"Dear God, I've got your mama. If you want her back, you WILL send me a red bicycle for my birthday."

THE HAIRCUT

A young boy had just gotten his driving permit. He asked his father, who was a minister if they could discuss the use of the car. His father took him to the study and said, "Let's make a deal, you bring up your grades, study your bible and get your hair cut and we will talk about it."

In a month, the boy came back and asked if they could discuss the use of the car. They again went to the study and the father said, "Son, I am very proud of you. You've brought your grades up, you've studied your Bible diligently, but you didn't get your hair cut."

The young man paused for a moment, then said, "You know Dad, I've been thinking about that. Samson had long hair, Moses had long hair, Noah had long hair, and even Jesus had long hair..."

His father replied, "Yes, and they walked everywhere they went!"

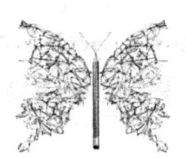

Chapter 9

"LIFE PICKUPS FROM BRAZIL LIKE THE COUNTRY"

One of my hobbies is taking notes. I always carry a notepad. I take notes anywhere a sermon or a lesson is being given (i.e. Churches, seminars, funerals, TV, or just anything I hear that is profound). Taking notes enables you to capture anything that touched your spirit enough for you to recall later.

Reading your notes can be thought-provoking, calming, and a mind cleansing experience. Writing and sharing my *Life Pickups* gives me joy.

From great minds come great thoughts. Thank you for allowing me to share some of my favorites:

I CAN DO ALL THINGS THROUGH CHRIST, WHO STRENGTHENS ME

Bible, Philippians 4:13

LIVE ONE DAY AT A TIME (LODAAT)

Jay Khatau

IF YOU ARE NOT BEING MOVED BY YOUR INNER POWER, YOU'RE BEING PUSHED AND NO ONE WANTS TO BE PUSHED

Rev. Matthew Reed

MIRACLES ARE GOD'S BEST OR BRING YOU GOD'S BEST

Rev. Carlton Pearson

NO ONE CAN MAKE YOU FEEL INFERIOR WITHOUT YOUR CONSENT

Eleanor Roosevelt

POSITIVE THINKING IS REACTING POSITIVELY TO A NEGATIVE SITUATION

Bill Haven

THE GREATEST POWER THAT A PERSON POSSESSES, IS THE POWER TO CHOOSE

J. Martin Kohe

I GIVE THANKS TO MY HEAVENLY FATHER

Sharon Thomas

I BELIEVE THAT YOU CAN GET EVERYTHING YOU WANT IF YOU WILL JUST HELP ENOUGH OTHER PEOPLE GET WHAT THEY WANT

Zig Zigler

YOU LEAVE A PART OF YOU EVERYWHERE YOU GO

Bishop Carlton Pearson

*DON'T TALK ABOUT THE WAY YOU ARE
TALK ABOUT THE WAY YOU WANT TO BE*

Rev. Joel Osteen

*INJUSTICE ANYWHERE IS A THREAT
TO JUSTICE EVERYWHERE*

Martin Luther King

*I DON'T CARE WHO KNOWS WHERE I'VE BEEN
AS LONG AS I DON'T FORGET IT*

Captain Mark Stevenson

I AM MORE THAN JUST A CONQUEROR

Rev. Joel Osteen

IT'S NOT OVER UNTIL YOU WIN

Les Brown

*IF YOU MAKE SOMEONE ELSE'S DAY
GOD WILL MAKE YOURS*

Rev. Joel Osteen

*THERE IS NOTHING EITHER GOOD OR BAD,
BUT THINKING MAKES IT SO*

William Shakespeare

*THINGS TURN OUT BEST FOR THE PEOPLE WHO
MAKE THE BEST OF THE WAY THINGS TURN OUT*

John Wooden

*EVERY FAILURE BRINGS WITH IT
THE SEED OF AN EQUIVALENT*

Napoleon Hill

*EVERYTHING HAS A CRACK IN IT.
THAT'S HOW LIGHT GETS IN*

Leonard Cohen

IF MUSIC BE THE FOOD OF LOVE, PLAY ON

William Shakespeare

ALWAYS THINK IN TERMS OF WHAT THE OTHER PERSON WANTS

James Van Fleet

DON'T SWEAT THE SMALL STUFF

Richard Carlson

SUCCESS RUNS IN OUR RACE

George C. Fraser

FOCUS ON WHAT YOU HAVE RATHER THAN WHAT YOU HAD

Suze Orman

THE JOB OF THE SOUL IS TO SURRENDER

Rev. Gaylon McDowell

UNDERSTAND THERE'S NO SUCH THING AS A COINCIDENCE WHEN YOUR LIFE IS DIRECTED BY GOD

Rev. Joel Osteen

ALL THINGS ARE AVAILABLE TO ME THE MOMENT I THINK THEM

Rev. Derrick Wells

THE ONLY POWER ANYONE HAS OVER US IS WHAT WE GIVE AWAY

Rev. Gaylon McDowell

WHEN GOD IS ON THE INSIDE, HE SHOWS UP ON THE OUTSIDE

Bishop Dewayne Funches

THE ONLY THING YOU REALLY KNOW IS WHAT YOU HAVE EXPERIENCED

Bishop Carlton Pearson

IT WORKS IF YOU WORK IT

Rev. Johnnie Coleman

BEST CAN BE BEATEN BY BETTER

Bishop Carlton Pearson

ALWAYS LOOK FOR THE GREATER GOOD IN EVERYTHING

Julian Nettles-Bey

I PRAY AND GO WITH THE FLOW

Vivian C. Brazil

BECOME THE FLOW

Gina Pearson

I CAN CHANGE THINGS IN MY LIFE

Rev. Roderick Norton

LOVE IS NOT WHAT IT SAYS, IT'S WHAT IT DOES

Simon T. Bailey

ALL CAUSATION IS MENTAL

Rev. Derrick Wells

YOU MUST BE DEFINITE WITH THE INFINITE

Rev. Ike

I REALIZE THAT THE GREATEST LOVE AFFAIR I'LL EVER HAVE IS THE ONE WITH MYSELF

Cherilyn Azubuike

FOES CANNOT STOP YOU FROM YOUR DESTINY

Rev. Lenell Jackson

WHAT WILL YOUR LEGACY BE?

Dr. Margaret Burroughs

YOUR DESTINY IS IN YOUR HANDS

President Barack Obama

KNOWLEDGE BREEDS CONFIDENCE THAT IS BACKED BY SUBSTANCE

Dr. Kenneth Lewis Sr.

YOU CAN OVERCOME EVERY OBSTACLE, NO MATTER WHAT

Lisa Nichols

THE WAY YOU TREAT YOURSELF, TELLS OTHER PEOPLE HOW TO TREAT YOU

Rev. Ike

GOD HELPS THEM THAT HELP THEMSELVES

Benjamin Franklin

LOVE CONQUERS ALL THINGS

Virgil

NEVER PUT A QUESTION MARK WHERE GOD HAS PUT A PERIOD

Rev. Joel Osteen

CREATIVITY IS PART OF YOUR MYSTICAL SELF

Rev. Roderick Norton

TRUSTING THAT THERE WILL BE A GOOD OUTCOME ALLOWS YOU TO THINK MORE CLEARLY

Lisa Nichols

SELF LOVE IS POSITIVE SELF-ESTEEM

Rev. Ike

WE ASSOCIATE UP TO LEARN AND ASSOCIATE DOWN TO TEACH

Joe "Mr. Network" Pelayo

WHATEVER I HAVE, I HAVE BY RIGHT OF CONSCIOUSNESS

Rev. Roderick Norton

EVERYTHING IS OK
NOTHING SEPARATES TIME BUT NOW

King Solomon

BEING A REAL MAN IS NOT DETERMINED FROM
THE WAIST DOWN, BUT FROM THE NECK UP

Dr. Steven Thurston

EVERY SITUATION IS BASED ON GIVING AND
RECEIVING

Ethel Russell-Ajisomo

LET YOUR INTUITION BE YOUR GUIDE

Oprah Winfrey

THE MANNER IN WHICH WE LIVE
INFLUENCES OUR ATTITUDE TOWARD DEATH

Delano O'Banion

*A PROMISE DRIVEN LIFE IS NOT ONLY FRUITFUL,
IT HELPS OTHERS BEAR FRUIT*

Dr. Therman E. Evans

KNOW WHEN TO SPEAK UP AND WHEN TO SHUT UP

Dr. Michael Sedler

EXPERIENCE ALLOWS NO DROPOUTS

Beverly Thompson

*LOVING YOURSELF IS NOT ABOUT BEING SELFISH,
IT'S ABOUT HONORING GOD'S CREATION...YOU*

Victoria Osteen

*THERE IS NO SUCH THING AS "NOTHINGS NEW",
EVERY PASSING MOMENT MAKES THAT TRUE*

Ardencia

*WHEN PEOPLE TELL YOU WHO THEY ARE,
BELIEVE THEM BECAUSE THEY KNOW THEMSELVES
BETTER THAN YOU*

Maya Angelou

*INSTEAD OF WAITING FOR AN OPPORTUNITY
TO KNOCK, KICK THE DOOR IN*

Tom Joyner

*WATCH YOUR DEEDS AND GUIDE YOUR FEET,
ALWAYS PRACTICE WHAT YOU PREACH*

Verlie Cambric

*IF YOU WANT THE HOOK UP
YOU GOT TO PICK A BOOK UP*

Dr. Winston Johnson

*THE LAW OF COMMAND IS TO COMMAND
MY GOOD TO COME FORTH*

Rev. Sheila McKeithen

MY PROVISION BEGINS IN MY CONSCIOUSNESS

Rev. Roderick Norton

*WHEN LIFE KNOCKS YOU DOWN,
SAY THANK YOU THEN GET UP*

Carolann Jones

THE GREATNESS OF A MAN IS IN HIS INTEGRITY AND HIS ABILITY TO AFFECT THOSE AROUND HIM POSITIVELY

Bob Marley

BEING IS BECOMING THE THING

Rev. Gwindol P. Tate

SEND NEGATIVE THOUGHTS AN EVICTION NOTICE

Rev. Helen Carry

LOVE YOURSELF ENOUGH TO FEEL THAT YOU DESERVE THE BEST

Rev. Evelyn Boyd

IF YOU DON'T LOVE, FORGIVE, AND RESPECT YOURSELF, HOW DO YOU EXPECT IT OF OTHERS?

Bishop Carlton Pearson

*YOU HAVE BEEN EQUIPPED FOR THE RACE
SPECIFICALLY DESIGNED FOR YOU*

Rev. Joel Osteen

*LOVE PEOPLE WHERE YOU FIND THEM, NOT WHERE
YOU WISH THEY WERE AND START WITH YOURSELF*

Minister Rick Williams

*YOUR TIME IS LIMITED, SO DON'T WASTE IT
LIVING SOMEONE ELSE'S LIFE.
STAY HUNGRY, STAY FOOLISH*

Steve Jobs

*AS WE ANSWER OUR CALL TO GREATNESS,
WE ARE IN THE FLOW*

Rev. James Trapp

*YOU CAN'T ACCOMPLISH ANYTHING
WITHOUT THANKING SOMEONE*

Terry Bradshaw

ALWAYS STRIVE TO MAKE A DIFFERENCE, BE UNIQUE

Rick Beluggo

IT'S NOT WHERE YOU START IN LIFE IT'S WHERE YOU END UP

Colin Powell

COMMIT TO EXCELLENCE, BE GOOD AT WHAT YOU DO. FOCUS ON DEVELOPING A SKILL

Brian Tracy

TODAY'S READERS ARE TOMORROWS LEADERS

Debra German

PAY ATTENTION TO WHAT YOU NOTICE AND WHY DID YOU NOTICE IT

Bishop Carlton Pearson

IF YOUR WORD IS NO GOOD, NEITHER ARE YOU

Zig Zigler

***BEHAVIOR REFLECTS ATTITUDE.
BEFORE THERE IS A CHANGE IN BEHAVIOR
THERE MUST BE A CHANGE IN ATTITUDE***

Charles Hamilton

**PAY ATTENTION TO THE LITTLE THINGS.
THEY PAY OFF**

Joe Montana

***GOD PUTS PEOPLE IN YOUR LIFE EVERY DAY
TO BLESS YOU***

James Smith

***IT IS IMPORTANT TO GET CHILDREN TO TELL YOU
WHAT THEY WANT TO BE***

Rudy Giuliani

COACHING IS TEACHING

Mike Ditka

IN LIFE, WHAT YOU SEE DEPENDS ON
WHERE YOU ARE SITTING

Steven Pierce

WHERE YOU SPEND YOUR MONEY,
YOU ARE CREATING JOBS

Webb Evans

EVERYONE NEEDS TO LEAVE SOMETHING BEHIND
FOR OTHERS TO WORK WITH

Rev. Marvin E. Wiley

IT'S A WONDERFUL THING TO KNOW GOD,
ESPECIALLY BEFORE A SITUATION

Rev. Paulette Smith

DON'T TAKE MATTERS INTO YOUR OWN HANDS.
PRAY FOR GUIDANCE IN EVERYTHING

Rev. Lamont Sherrill

YOU ALWAYS PAY FOR GOOD ACCOUNTING
ONE WAY OR ANOTHER

Ted Hollander

*IT'S BETTER TO HAVE AND NOT NEED, THAN
TO NEED AND NOT HAVE*

Joseph Taylor

HE WHO HAS A WHY CAN DEAL WITH ANY HOW

Robert M. Pairs

*LOVE IS THE GREATEST INVESTMENT
NO MATTER WHO YOU GIVE IT TO*

Cuttie W. Bacon III, Ph.D

THE MORE IT HURTS, THE MORE YOU SHOULD LOVE

Rev. Sun Myung Moon

*THE MORE PEOPLE YOU INFLUENCE
THE MORE POWER YOU HAVE*

G. Drew Williams

YOU CAN GIVE YOUR WAY OUT OF DEBT

Bishop Carlton Pearson

DOING WHAT YOU LOVE MEANS DEALING WITH THINGS YOU DON'T

David Shore

GOD IS ABOUT TO MAKE YOU LAUGH (LIKE SARAH)

Dr. Sean McMillan

OUR INNER ATTITUDE DOES NOT HAVE TO REFLECT OUR OUTER CIRCUMSTANCES

Rev. Samuel Mendenhall

SUCCESS IS A GROUP ENDEAVOR

Donna Billinger

REALIZATION CREATES A MOVEMENT. YOU CAN'T GO BACK

Rev. Gaylon McDowell

RESPECT COMMANDS ITSELF AND CAN NEITHER BE GIVEN, NOR WITHHELD WHEN IT IS DUE

Eldridge Cleaver

WHEN GOD MAKES A FOOL HE MAKES A PERFECT ONE

Richard Pryor

I PLAY THE BEST MUSIC OF YOUR LIFE

Richard Pegue

WHEN YOU CAN'T SLEEP, YOU SHOULD LISTEN

Bishop Carlton Pearson

GOD IS ALWAYS SPEAKING

Bishop William Ellis

PRACTICE THE PRINCIPLES TO GET THE OUTCOME

Pastor Greg Stanton

JOYFUL PEOPLE ARE A GIFT FROM GOD

Rev. P. Devon Brown

I AM BOTH A CHRISTIAN AND A MUSLIM

Minister Louis Farrakhan

GIVE DRIVE BY PRAYERS

Dr. La'Vel F. Hardy

DIRECTION IS MORE IMPORTANT THAN SPEED

Berry Gordy Jr.

IF THE ONLY PRAYER YOU EVER SAY IS 'THANK YOU' IT IS ENOUGH

Oprah Winfrey

DREAM, BUT DON'T SLEEP

Dr. Ashley Walls

WHAT IS THE BIGGEST ROOM IN THE WORLD? THE ROOM FOR IMPROVEMENT

William Hooks, Sr.

WHEN COURAGE IS NOT ENOUGH BRING YOUR "A" GAME

William Dock Walls

THERE'S A PREACHER FOR EVERY CREATURE

Rev. T. L. Barrett

AWARENESS IS EVERYTHING

Vivian Brazil

THERE CAN BE NO BIRTH WITHOUT LABOR, SO BIRTH THAT BOOK

J.D. Cooper

KNOW WHEN TO STOP BEFORE YOU START®

Horseshoe Casino

IT ALWAYS SEEMS IMPOSSIBLE UNTIL IT'S DONE

Nelson Mandela

WHEN YOU HEAR THE TRUTH YOU HAVE TO SAY, AMEN

Rev. Otis Moss

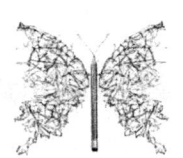

Chapter 10
APPENDIX

EXHIBIT 1

In 2003, Paul was one of two students from Beasley Elementary Magnate Academic Center in Chicago, selected to have their poems published.

Exhibit 2

By 2004, my grandson Mario's had several medals for demonstrating his athletic abilities in track and field. The image below shows only a few of them.

EXHIBIT 3

Presidents Bill Clinton and Barack Obama thanking me for my volunteering. In 2012, I was a telephone Bank Coordinator for President Obama's Campaign. When we completed the campaign, I received this personalized autographed photo from Bill Clinton and President Barack Obama.

Exhibit 4
Inaugural Invitation

To my surprise, as a result of my volunteer work, I received a great perk, an invitation to the Presidents inaugural ball after his re-election in 2013.

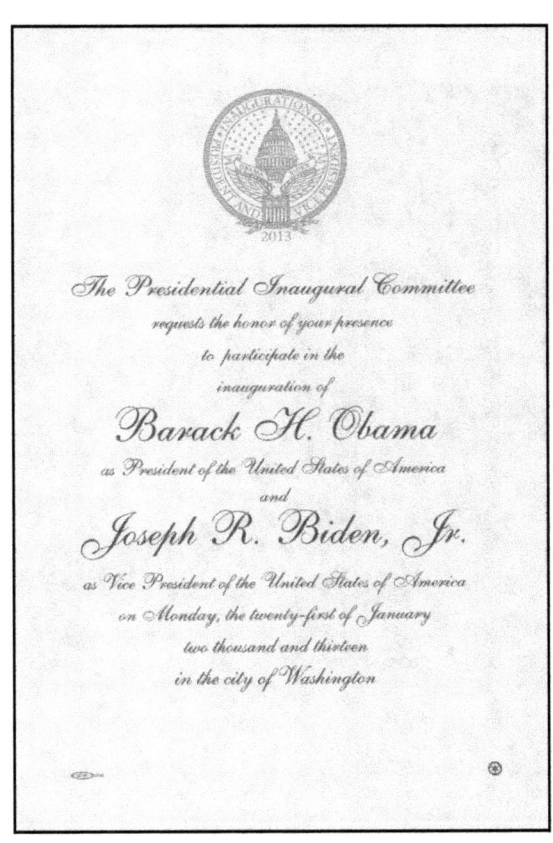

EXHIBIT 5

I received this after my participation as a telephone bank coordinator in President Obama's 2nd campaign for President. Bo's paw print, nice touch Mr. President.

Exhibit 6

As a member of the U. S. Postal Service Women's Program Committee, I helped plan organize and attended numerous Career Awareness Conferences. I strongly believe in self enhancement and sharing knowledge.

EXHIBIT 7

I went to San Francisco CA, for a 4 day extensive training as a lead trainer for the Mail Classification Reform.

DISTRICT MANAGER
CENTRAL ILLINOIS DISTRICT

 **UNITED STATES POSTAL SERVICE**

January 31, 1997

Ms. Vivian C. Brazil
6630 South Morgan Street
Chicago, IL 60621-1226

Dear Ms. Brazil:

It is a pleasure to congratulate you for having earned this Special Achievement Award, letter and cash award for the above average performance of assigned duties.

Vivian, you are one of the individuals who worked on the training team for Classification Reform and did so in an exemplary manner while in most instances performing your regular duty assignment. As a member of the training team, you successfully trained almost 5000 customers and 1500 employees during 254 separate sessions. A phenomenal amount of time and effort went into the success of this training effort, while very little revenue was spent on supplies, services and travel. Without question, your personal dedication, enthusiasm and energy devoted to this project contributed to the precedent-setting success of Classification Reform implementation.

A copy of this award letter has been furnished for your Official Personnel Folder to serve as a permanent record of your accomplishment. It will, therefore, be helpful to you throughout your Postal Career.

Sincerely,

J. R. Olden, Jr.

/kab

Enclosure

Delivering Excellence...Every Step of the Way!

Exhibit 8

From 1994 through 1998, I was the U. S. Postal Service Standard Mail Classification Course classroom instructor and taught a total of 58 students. They had to pass a test in order to qualify for the position of Bulk Mail Acceptance Clerk. When I started, there was a 50% failing rate. I raised the rate it to 99% passing and received a Special Achievement Award shown below.

Exhibit 9
Letter of appreciation from The International Stevenson Foundation

I joined The ISF as a volunteer and through interaction with those who were offenders and in recovery, I motivated, inspired and assisted the operation of the foundation. I eventually became the director of the agency.

EXHIBIT 10

Clara's House Plaque

I received this award, "Volunteer of the Year" for being a listening ear to homeless and battered women. In order to motivate and inspire women, I would play motivational tapes from Reverend Ike and Les Brown. I would also read various volumes of Reverend Johnnie Coleman's book series titled, "It Works If You Work It" to the women and their children.

EXHIBIT 11

In October of 1997 I made history by participating in first and only Million Woman March. I united with other African American women across the nation to inspire our communities to work for their own improvement. The march, was organized by Phile Chionesu and Asia Coney, two Philadelphia grass roots activists,

EXHIBIT 12

A special appreciation for my contribution to the Classification Reform Training Project.

Exhibit 13

From 1994 through 1998, I was the U. S. Postal Service Standard Mail Classification Course classroom instructor and taught a total of 58 students. They had to pass a test in order to qualify for the position of Bulk Mail Acceptance Clerk. When I started, there was a 50% failing rate. I raised the rate to 99% passing and received a Special Achievement Award. This certificate of appreciation was presented to me by one of my classes after they passed their exam.

Certificate of Appreciation

Presented to

Ms. Vivian C. Brazil
Bulk Mail Acceptance Instructor
Central District - South Surburban
United States Postal Service
Bedford Park, IL 60499

Signed

[signatures]

March 24th, 1995

Exhibit 14

Federal Employee Nominee for Community Service Award

Volunteering has offered me an opportunity to serve my community. When I received this award from the Postal Service for the valuable time, I spent assisting the women at Clara's House it was an extra bonus.

2000 FEDERAL EMPLOYEE OF THE YEAR AWARDS PROGRAM

Honors

Vivian C. Brazil
U.S. Postal Service

Nominee

Outstanding Community Service Employee
Chicago Metropolitan Area

In Recognition Of Outstanding Contribution To The Federal Service Through Exemplary Job Performance

Chair, Employee of the Year Committee

Chair, Chicago Federal Executive Board

I Just Want To Share

EXHIBIT 15

Santa Envelope letter

Letter of Appreciation for the suggestion of adding an image of Santa to the return address on the envelope.

LEAD EXECUTIVE
DISTRICT MANAGER, CUSTOMER SERVICE AND SALES
CENTRAL ILLINOIS PERFORMANCE CLUSTER

UNITED STATES POSTAL SERVICE

January 5, 2001

Vivian Brazil
Central Illinois District

Dear Ms. Brazil:

CONGRATULATIONS! This letter and monetary gift recognizes your outstanding idea proposal.

Your suggestion to include a picture of Santa Claus along with a customized return address on the envelopes of our Santa letters, was an excellent idea. By doing so, young children who are unable to read can tell when Santa's letter has arrived. Additionally, letters deemed undeliverable can be returned to Consumer Affairs for address correction.

The fond and memorable holiday tradition of sending and receiving Santa letters was enhanced by your creativity. This letter and small gift serves as a token of appreciation for your idea.

A copy of this Letter of Recognition will be placed in your Official Personnel Folder as a permanent record of your accomplishment.

Sincerely,

James M. Holmes
James M. Holmes

Enclosure

/nm:9631

6801 W. 73RD STREET
BEDFORD PARK IL 60499-9998
708 563-7800
FAX 708 563-2013

EXHIBIT 16

Santa Envelope

I received an award for my suggestion to add a picture of Santa from the North Pole on the return address of letters being sent back to children who sent letters to Santa.

Exhibit 17

My joy has always been in attending various self-enhancement seminars including "Breakthrough" with Tony Brown, "The One Decision" with Judith Wright, and currently I am attending the "Landmark Forum."

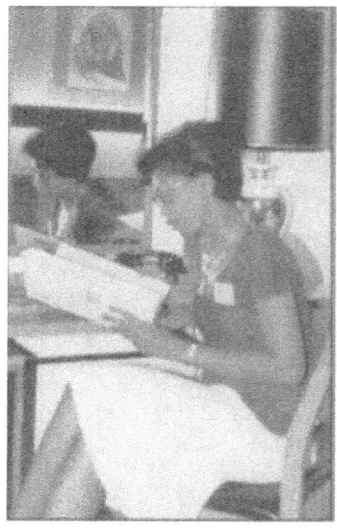

EXHIBIT 18

Rev. Matthew Reed Letter of Appreciation

I was awarded this for assisting Rev. Reed with several of his Matthew Reed Crusade (MRC) Growth Seminars.

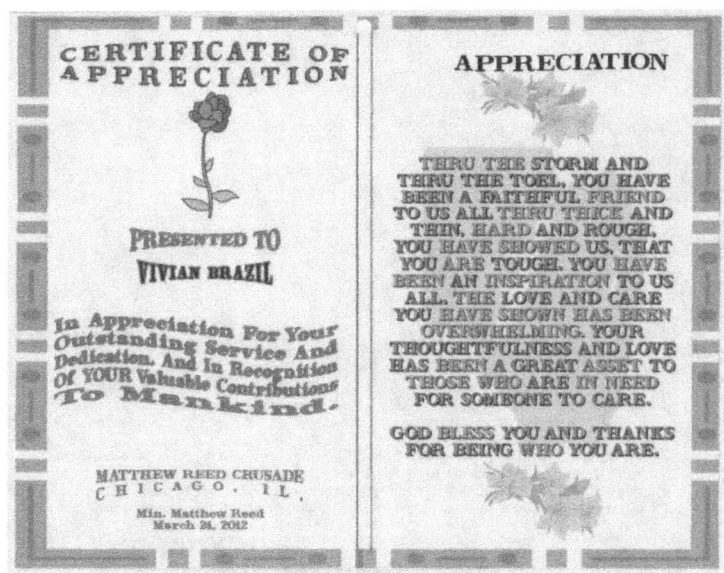

I Just Want To Share

Exhibit 19

Letter for becoming a nominee for Federal Employee of the year

The Director of Marketing submitted my name for my exemplary service within the department. Also, for volunteering for extra assignments and committees within the United States Postal Service.

J. T. WEEKER
VICE PRESIDENT GREAT LAKES AREA OPERATIONS

UNITED STATES POSTAL SERVICE

July 29, 1996

Vivian C. Brazil
Business Mail Entry
Central Illinois District

Dear Ms. C. Brazil:

I wanted to send you a personal congratulations for receiving the Federal Employee Award nomination. I know that you must have felt a sense of appreciation and pleasure in realizing that your fellow employees recognize your efforts and contribution to our organization.

I was disappointed that not a single postal employee made it to the final round of the awards process let alone to not have had a postal employee win in any of the nine categories. I have asked that we receive detailed information regarding the selection process to help us be better prepared for next year's award program. It is clear to me that postal people merit more serious consideration and I am committed to making sure they receive it.

I look forward to chairing the awards ceremony next year, and again, I want to express my sincerest appreciation for your contribution to our organization.

Sincerely,

J. T. Weeker

500 EAST FULLERTON AVENUE
CAROL STREAM, IL 60199-5555
708/260-5555

EXHIBIT 20

1996 Nominee for "Federal Employee of the Year"

It was an honor to be a nominee for Federal Employee of the Year. My motto in life is to do the best in every area of life. It may not be the best but it will make it in the top 10.

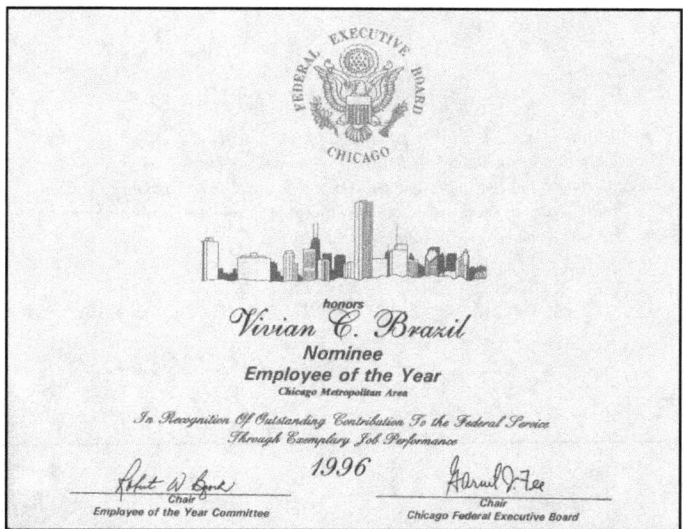

Exhibit 21

Mom's birthday card for her 90th birthday from the Obamas with envelope.

THE WHITE HOUSE
WASHINGTON

We are pleased to join your family and friends in wishing you the best on your birthday. Your generation has shown the courage to persevere through moments of uncertainty and challenge, and your story is an important part of the American narrative. We hope you look back with joy and pride on the many contributions and memories made over the course of your life.

We wish you health and happiness in the years ahead.

Sincerely,

[signed] Barack Obama   Michelle Obama

THE WHITE HOUSE
WASHINGTON, DC 20500

Mrs. Ruth Webb

Chicago, Illinois 60621

EXHIBIT 22

Mom's thank you for your support card from the Obamas.

To Ruth,
Movements for real and lasting change are sustained by the relationships we build with one another.
Thank you for your support.

Michelle Obama

I Just Want To Share

Exhibit 23

Letter of appreciation for Bowling for Charity

Letter for outstanding leadership for the Bowling for Charity fundraising event. The Central Illinois District Postal Service brought home the trophy out of four districts.

LEAD EXECUTIVE
DISTRICT MANAGER, CUSTOMER SERVICE AND SALES
CENTRAL ILLINOIS PERFORMANCE CLUSTER

UNITED STATES POSTAL SERVICE

November 28, 2000

Vivian C. Brazil
Mailing Requirements Clerk
Central Illinois District

Dear Vivian,

This Certificate of Appreciation is in recognition of your outstanding leadership in the coordination of the 3rd Annual Bowling Challenge. As lead coordinator for the Central Illinois District, you made a major contribution to the success and ultimate winning of the trophy. The acceptance of this trophy was one of my proudest moments.

It was gratifying to see so many employees at all levels come together for such a good cause, to raise funds for the Combined Federal Campaign (CFC). The extra efforts displayed by everyone working together with mutual respect and harmony were significant and personified camaraderie.

Your planning, organizing, advertising and motivating employees with the air of competition made this event very successful. Our contribution to the CFC, as a result of this function was $1500.00. This was an increase of $500.00 over last year.

Please accept the enclosed $25.00 gift cards, for a total value of $100.00, as a token of the appreciation for donating your time and energy to this endeavor.

A copy of this letter will be placed in your Official Personnel Folder to serve as a permanent record of your leadership and motivational abilities exhibited during the coordination of this event.

Sincerely,

Ronald D Crozen
For James M. Holmes

/vcb9651

OPF

6801 W. 73RD STREET
BEDFORD PARK IL 60499-9998
708 563-7600
FAX 708 563-2013

Vivian Brazil

EXHIBIT 24

Bowling for Charity

As an avid bowler since 1972 this project was right up my alley (Pun intended). It was my pleasure to organize and participate in this CFC fundraiser.

Bowling for dollars

The 3rd Annual Illinois District Challenge Bowling for Charity event netted $5,000 to be donated to the Combined Federal Campaign by the Chicago, Central Illinois, and Northern Illinois Districts, and the Great Lakes Area Office. Participants bowled in two shifts at Miami Bowl (5023 South Archer Ave.). Each district had two teams in the championship round. The final round consisted of one game, winner takes all. The winning district team—Central Illinois (pictured above)—posted the highest combined score from their two teams and will display the championship trophy for one year. (photos by James Dillard Jr.)

Holiday news? Please...send it in time to be included in the January 2001 UPDATE
The January 2001 Great Lakes Area UPDATE will feature holiday "wrap-up" stories. Please use the story report form on page 11 to send in your holiday news by Jan. 8.

8 • December 2000

Exhibit 25

This award was presented for my participation with the Women's Program Committee in Super South Bad, which was a dance routine to the tune of Michael Jackson's "BAD".

Exhibit 26

During my 35 years of service at the Post Office, I was a member of the American Postal Workers Union, Local 6591. For a brief period of time I was the Treasurer.

Exhibit 27

I Thank God for my 35 years of service at the South Suburban District Postal Service in Bedford Park IL.

Conclusion

I hope that in reading *"I JUST WANT TO SHARE,"* you have been enlightened, inspired, motivated, humored, and blessed. My desire is that you have had as much fun reading it, as I had in writing it. I hope there were some things that gave you ideas that will enhance your life. I hope you had some good laughs, and enjoyed this book. God Bless You!

The book may be ordered at www.vivbrazil.com. Vivian Brazil is available for book signings upon request. She may be reached via e-mail: brazilwanttoshare@yahoo.com.

www.ingramcontent.com/pod-product-compliance
Lightning Source LLC
Chambersburg PA
CBHW050342010526
44119CB00049B/663